**Walkthrough**

Let's read the title page, 'The Troll from the Mill'.

 **Phonic Opportunity**

Point to the words 'Troll' and 'Mill' and say them, pointing out the double consonants at the end of the words make one sound.

Walkthrough

Point to 'mill' in the text and picture, and explain what it is.

What is the troll wearing? Where is he going?

The troll from the mill . . .

2

Observe and Prompt

Word Recognition

(P) Check children are using their decoding skills to read the words 'mill', 'ran', 'up' and 'hill', sounding out and blending through each word to read it. If they struggle with 'troll', model how to sound out and blend this word.

- Can the children find and read the high frequency words 'The' and 'from'?

ran up the hill.

3

Observe and Prompt

Language Comprehension

- Check that the children understand what a mill is and who the troll is.

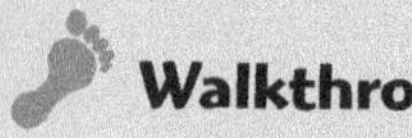

Walkthrough

How is the troll feeling now?

Observe and Prompt

Word Recognition

P Encourage the children to use their decoding skills to read the words on these two pages, including 'huff' and 'puff', but help them with these words if they struggle.

P Ask children what they notice about the words 'huff' and 'puff'.

Walkthrough

Who can this be? Point to the horns.

5

Observe and Prompt

Language Comprehension

- Check that the children are able to comment on what is happening in the story and make a guess about who the horns belong to.

Walkthrough

This is Big Boss the Bull. He looks very angry. Why?
What do you think he might say to the troll?

Observe and Prompt

Word Recognition

P Check that children continue to use their decoding skills
to read the CVC words, sounding out and blending all
through the words.

● The word 'saw' is a high frequency word, but children may be
unable to decode it at this stage. If they struggle, tell them
this word and model how to read it.

"Buzz off!" said Big Boss.

7

Observe and Prompt

Language Comprehension

- Check that the children understand or can guess why the bull might be angry.
- Encourage them to read 'Buzz off!' in an angry voice.

9

 **Walkthrough**

What has Big Boss the Bull done to the poor troll?

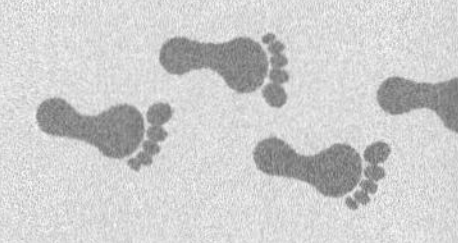

 **Observe and Prompt**

Word Recognition

P Check that the children can use their decoding skills to sound out and blend through the words 'troll', 'from', 'mill', 'back' and 'hill'.

● If children struggle to decode the words 'rolled' and 'down', tell them these words and model how to sound out and blend them. Ask children to spot the double 'l' in 'rolled'.

10

Revisit and Respond

- Read the story again to a partner.
- Role-play the story in pairs, using props (horns, masks, etc.).
- Use magnetic letters to make all the words ending with double letters.

Independent Group Activity Work

This book is accompanied by two photocopy masters, one with a reading focus, and one with a writing focus, which support the teaching objectives for this book. The photocopy masters can be found in the *Star Planning and Assessment Guide*.

PCM Ph2.1 (reading)

PCM Ph2.2 (writing)

You may also like to invite the children to read the story again, during their independent reading (either at school or at home).

ASSESSMENT POINTS

Assess that the children have learnt the main teaching focus of this book by checking that they can:

Word Recognition	Language Comprehension
• use decoding skills to read the whole story, especially words ending with consonant digraphs ('troll', 'mill', 'hill', 'buzz', 'boss', 'bull').	• explain what the troll does in the story and why the events happen; • talk about what is happening on each page.